A1 MIRACLES FOR

God will strenghten
your hands
and help you with
many divine
assignments he
has for you.

David Ayesuyaps

THE
ATMOSPHERE
MIRACLES FOR

DAVID AYESIYENGA

TATE PUBLISHING
AND **ENTERPRISES, LLC**

Published by Tate Publishing & Enterprises, LLC
127 E. Trade Center Terrace | Mustang, Oklahoma 73064 USA
1.888.361.9473 | www.tatepublishing.com

Tate Publishing is committed to excellence in the publishing industry. The company reflects the philosophy established by the founders, based on Psalm 68:11,
"The Lord gave the word and great was the company of those who published it."

Book design copyright © 2015 by Tate Publishing, LLC. All rights reserved.
Cover design by Joana Quilantang
Interior design by Richell Balansag

Published in the United States of America

ISBN: 978-1-68207-905-8
1. Religion / General
2. Religion / Christian Life / General
15.09.03

CONTENTS

BE THANKFUL TO GOD

THANKSGIVING CREATES AN ATMOSPHERE FOR MIRACLES

An atmosphere for a miracle begins with the act of thanksgiving. We have to be thankful to God for everything and for every situation. It will create the atmosphere for miracles in our lives. We are admonished in 1 Thessalonians 5:16 to remain thankful to God for everything that happens in our lives. We need to thank God for little blessings and for big blessings. If we cannot be faithful to thank God for little blessings, then we should not expect God to commit into our hands big blessings.

Jesus thanked God for the seven loaves of bread and few fishes received from his disciples. That created an atmosphere for the miraculous multiplication of those few fishes and seven loaves of bread to feed over four thousand people. It is recorded in the Bible that there was a surplus gathered after that miracle.

> And Jesus saith unto them, How many loaves have ye? And they said, Seven, and a few little fishes. And he commanded the multitude to sit down on the grass, and he took the seven loaves, and the fishes, and gave thanks, he blessed, and brake them, and gave to his disciples, and the disciples to the multitude, And they did all eat, and were filled: and they took up of the broken meat that was left seven baskets full. And they that eat were four thousand men, beside women and children. (Matt. 15:34–38)

Thank God for whatever you have now. It will create an atmosphere for multiplication. Thank God for the one door the Lord has opened for you. It will move him to open more doors for you.

Jesus was always thankful to God for every situation. He thanked God at the tomb of Lazarus, creating an atmosphere for the miraculous resurrection of Lazarus.

> Then they took away the stone from the place where the dead was laid. And Jesus lifted up his eyes, and said, Father, I thank thee that thou hast heard me. And I knew that thou hearest me

always; but because of the people which stand by I said it, that they may believe that thou hast sent me. And when he thus had spoken, he cried with a loud voice, Lazarus, come forth. (John 11:41–43, KJV)

Another account worth mentioning is the ten lepers that Jesus healed. It is recorded in the Bible that only one leper came back to thank Jesus after receiving that miracle. The other nine disappeared and could not be found. Do you know what Jesus did? He questioned the whereabouts of the other nine lepers who did not return. That means thanksgiving certainly is something that matters to God. Therefore, we cannot ignore the principle of thanksgiving if we desire to see an atmosphere for miracles. In appreciation of what that one leper did, Jesus made his life whole. That means Jesus said, "Because you were careful to thank me for healing, I will add to you all the other necessities of life." That word *whole* stands for total deliverance from everything.

And as he entered into a certain village, there met him ten men that were lepers, which stood afar off:

And they lifted up their voices, and said Jesus, Master, have mercy on us. And when he saw them, he said unto them, Go shew yourselves unto the priests. And it came to pass, that as they went, they were cleansed. And one of them, when he saw that he was healed, turned back, and with a loud voice glorified God. And fell down on his face at his feet, giving him thanks: and he was a Samaritan.

And Jesus answering said, Were there not ten cleansed? but where are the nine?

There are not found that returned to give glory to God, save this stranger. And he said unto him, Arise, go thy way; thy faith has made thee whole. (Luke 17:12–19, KJV)

If we cannot thank God for the free air we breathe, how do we expect him to heal our sick bodies? If we cannot thank God for healing us of bodily pains, how do we expect him to heal us of cancer? Thanksgiving creates the atmosphere for miracles, and we must learn to be thankful to God daily in order to see his miracles.

The psalmist knew the connection between thanksgiving and the atmosphere for miracles.

Enter into his gates with thanksgiving, and into his courts with praise: be thankful unto him, and bless his name. (Ps. 100:4, KJV)

Thanksgiving connects us to the gates of heavens. It ushers us into God's presence, and that atmosphere is what is required for a miracle.

THANK GOD FOR LITTLE THINGS

Thank God for little blessings. If God has given you a little drop of water, it is a great signal that he can give you an ocean. That reminds me about the story of Elijah and the little cloud of rain. After his Mount Carmel victory over the Baal prophets, he told King Ahab to get ready for an abundance of rain. At the time of this declaration, there had been drought on the land for three and half years. There was no sign of any clouds or rain then, but Elijah began to pray for rain. While continuing to pray, he asked his servant to check for any sign of a cloud of rain. After checking six times, the servant reported that he saw no sign, but Elijah encouraged him to check the seventh time. This time, the servant reported seeing a small cloud of rain. At that point, Elijah stopped the prayer, and thanked God for that little sign.

> So Ahab went up to eat and to drink. And Elijah went up to the top of Carmel, and cast himself down upon the earth, and put his face between his knees.
>
> And said to his servant, Go up now, look toward the sea. And he went up, and looked and said, there is nothing. And he said, Go again seven times.
>
> And it came to pass at the seventh time, that he said, Behold, there ariseth a little cloud out of the sea, like a man's hand. And he said, Go

up, say unto Ahab, Prepare thy chariots, and get thee down, that the rain stop thee not. (1 Kings 18:42–44)

A sign as seemingly little as a cloud of rain should be enough for us to start thanking God for the abundance of rain too. Despise not your little beginnings. Despise not the little things God does for you. Those little things are signs of the big things ahead, and it is just proper to be thankful to him. Remember, an ocean is usually formed out of little drops of rain, and every signpost points to something bigger than it.

Back in the 1960s, a man by the name of Fred Deluca started the Subway sandwich restaurant business with an initial capital of only a thousand dollars, which he borrowed from a friend. As little as this might have been, he was content with it. He thanked God for that little borrowed money, went on to start the business, and with time, it began to grow and expand. Today, his little company has grown to be the world's largest sandwich company with locations all over the world. As of 2011, the business has spread across the world, with 35,852 restaurants in ninety-eight countries and territories, with total revenue of $16.2 billion. What began in the state of Connecticut, United States, as a small restaurant birthed out of a little idea with a capital as small as a thousand dollars has ushered in millions. Those millions of dollars are birthed out of the little thousand dollars he started the business with. The secret to achieving big results in life, business, and any area of life is to be content with little results and prayerfully seek for more.

A pastor over a small congregation must be thankful to God for those few members, so the Lord will give him big numbers. Be thankful for the small offering and tithes coming into the church and this will create an atmosphere for God to lift his hand over your finances and multiply those "little" offerings into thousands and millions.

How will God know you are thankful? He knows it when you cease seeing your congregation as little, when you stop being discontent over the little numbers, and when you do away with murmurings and complaints. Remember, too many complaints and murmurings do no good to us but instead open a door for the destroyer to come into our life.

When a pastor cannot see anything good in his members, it is another sign of not being thankful to God for whatever he has given him. If all you can see in your members is negative, then your heart will be so poisoned about them, and no atmosphere can be created for any miracle. Learn to see the good things in people and thank God for that. It will open a door for the Lord to deal with the bad side of their lives.

Make thanksgiving part of your daily life. Begin your day with thanksgiving and end it with thanksgiving. It will create an atmosphere for miracles in your life.

THANK GOD FOR YOUR EMPLOYEES

Wherefore comfort yourselves together, and
edify one another, even as also ye do.

—1 Thessalonians 5:11 (KJV)

The boss of a company should be thankful to God for
the lives of his employees and for all they do. Learn to
appreciate their input and recognize their hard work,
dedication, and commitment. As a CEO, you can show
your employees a heart of thanksgiving through kind
words, words of appreciation, letters of recognition, and
awards. You can even organize thanksgiving dinners for
your employees and families at the end of the year as a
way of showing your appreciation to God for their lives.
This will create an environment for productivity and
increase. If you have nothing to thank God for in your
employees, and all you do is tear them with insults and
threats, you will soon create an atmosphere that is too
unhealthy for any miracle.

THANK GOD FOR PAINFUL SITUATIONS

For all the wells which his father's servants had
digged in the days of Abraham his father, the
Philistines had stopped them, and filled them with
earth. And Abimelech said unto Isaac; Go from

us, for thou art much mightier than we. And Isaac departed thence, and pitched his tent in the valley of Gerar, and dwelt there. And Isaac digged again the wells of the water, which they had digged in the days of Abraham his father; for the philistines had stopped them after the death of Abraham: and he called their names by which his father had called them. And Isaac's servants digged in the valley, and found there a well of springing water. And the herdmen of Gerar did strive with Isaac's herdman, saying, The water is ours: and he called the name of the well Esek; because they strove with him. And they digged another well, and strove for that also: and he called the name of it Sitnah. And he removed from thence, and digged another well; and for that they strove not: and he called the name of it Rehoboth; and he said, For now the Lord hath made room for us, and we shall be fruitful in the land.

—Genesis 26:15–22

Troublesome people can be a burden, and their actions cause us nothing but pain, but we still have to thank God for their lives. We have to remind ourselves that it is the Lord who allows the wicked into our lives for his own glory and purpose. As painful as their actions can be, God sometimes uses the wicked to fulfill his divine purpose in our lives and help get us to our place of destiny. That is the reason why we have to thank God for their lives.

There is a story of a certain man who lost his job as a pastor through the action of a troublesome deacon in his church. It was the norm of the church that the leaders cast a vote at a special board meeting every year to make a decision as to whether or not to keep the pastor at his job. If the vote favored the pastor, he maintains his job. Otherwise, he loses it. On one such board meeting, the elders and deacons of the church were in the middle of casting their votes. At the end of the process, only one vote was required from this last deacon for the pastor to maintain his job. Other deacons tried to persuade him into giving out his vote, but he vehemently refused. The pastor eventually lost the job and was asked by the church to leave.

In despair, shame, and pain, he moved out of that village to a city to begin new work for the Lord. The Lord prospered the work of his hands and honored him with a very big ministry in the city. Today, he is thankful to God for the life of that troublesome deacon who refused to support him with his vote to maintain his job as a village pastor. He says that if that one vote had not been denied him by that troublesome deacon, he could have remained a village pastor all his life. Though the action of that troublesome deacon had caused him pain, God simply used his actions to propel the pastor to his place of destiny. As long as we are in God's will, all things will work together for our good.

There are painful situations that the Lord allows into our lives because he wants to use such moments to get us out of our comfort zone and bring us to the place where we belong. Thank God for such situations, and thank God for the people involved.

One time in the history of the world, God allowed persecution on the early church as his way of spreading the Gospel. The apostles had become comfortable in Jerusalem, and persecution was God's only way of getting them out of that comfort zone. The persecution was not a good thing, but it was helpful in spreading the Word of God. Out of that persecution, Philip saw the glory of God in Samaria, and Simeon, the sorcerer, lost his demonic hold over the people of Samaria.

THANK GOD FOR YOUR PARTNER

So ought men to love their wives as their own bodies. He that loveth his wife loveth himself. For no man ever yet hated his own flesh; but nourisheth and cherisheth it, even as the Lord the church.

—Ephesians 5:28–29

In a marriage, spouses should be thankful to God for one another's lives. It is wrong to walk around with a feeling that your partner is privileged to have you in his or her life. Your spouse matters to you, just like you do to him or her. Thank God for the kind of wife or husband he has blessed you with. Learn to see the good qualities in your partner and thank God for that. Appreciate your partner daily and give him or her words of compliments for their strengths and words of encouragement for their weakness. Stop blaming God for the kind of partner he has given you. God could not have given you a better fit than that partner. Don't be deceived into thinking there is something better out there than what you have. If you are thankful to God for what he has given you, it will create an environment for God to step into your life with divine secrets that will help you make that partner the better person you want.

A thankful heart creates a thankful home. With a thankful home, God will make your home his home, and an atmosphere for miracles will be created. There is always something to be thankful to God for in life each second, each minute, each hour, and each day. Keep your eyes on those things and avoid dwelling on the negative. People who have nothing to thank God for have little or no business receiving any miracle from the Lord.

Another way to create an atmosphere for miracles is through praise and worship.

Praise and Worship

It came even to pass, as the trumpeters and singers were as one, to make one sound to be heard in praising and thanking the Lord; and when they lifted up their voice with the trumpets and cymbals and instruments of musick, and praised the Lord, saying, For he is good; for his mercy endureth forever: that then the house was filled with a cloud, even the house of the Lord.

—2 Chronicles 5:13, (KJV)

You can create an atmosphere for miracles through praise and worship. You can turn your test to a testimony through praise and worship. Praising and worshipping the Lord should not only be done when in church but wherever we are. Find a great worship and praise CD and enjoy it in the morning or while driving. You will create a wonderful atmosphere for the Lord to work a miracle. Good worship and praise in a church creates an atmosphere for miracles. I have heard testimonies of healings and miracles wrought by the Lord during praise and worship. I have heard about burdens of people lifted while enjoying a great worship time in their car or in bed. As a traveling pastor, I noticed a much better flow in the anointing through me in churches with a great worship team than those with a poor worship team. Praise and worship is certainly vital for a miracle in our lives, home, churches, etc.

There is a biblical account of Elisha and the three kings who came to seek divine direction from him. Elisha told them. "I am not anointed to prophecy now. I have no word from the Lord for you. However, you can create the atmosphere for that miracle by getting a musician to display some praise and worship." As they obeyed the instructions, the Spirit of the Lord came upon Elisha, and he began to prophecy:

> But now bring me a minstrel. And it came to pass, when the minstrel played, that the hand of the Lord came upon him. And he said, Thus saith the Lord, Make this valley full of ditches. (2 Kings 3:15–16, KJV)

The kind of atmosphere we create around us can either enhance the release of miracles or cause us not to receive anything at all.

You create an atmosphere for miracles in the church when you begin praise and worship while at home, while driving to church, and while getting into the doors of the church. Don't walk to church with an attitude that makes it look as though you are carrying a burden no one can bear or has ever borne. Don't stand in church watching others praise the Lord while you create the impression that you have nothing to praise God for. Get enthusiastic. Don't be a spectator. Be vibrant. Allow praise and worship to flow through your mouth to the Lord. It will create the atmosphere for your miracle.

David praised the Lord seven times every day. The mighty wall of Jericho, with all its complex human architecture, came down through the power of praise and worship. Chains broke, and prison doors opened as Paul and Silas prayed and worshipped God.

In the days of King Jehoshaphat, the Lord defeated his enemies through the power of praise and worship. Jehoshaphat did not need to fight with any weapon of war. All he did was set up praise and worship team, and the Lord took over the battle against his enemies.

> Ye shall not need to fight in this battle: set yourselves, stand ye still, and see the salvation of the Lord with you, O Judah and Jerusalem: fear not, nor be dismayed; tomorrow go out against them: for the Lord will be with you. (2 Chron. 20:17, KJV)

And when he had consulted with the people, he appointed singers unto the Lord, and that should praise the beauty of holiness, as they went out before the army and say, Praise the Lord; for his mercy endureth forever.

And when they began tossing and praise, the Lord set ambushments against the children of Ammon, Moab, and mount Seir, which were come against Judah, and they were smitten. (2 Chron. 20:21–22, KJV)

You see, when we pray, God sends down his angel with the answer, but when we praise and worship God, he comes down personally to deal with anything that is an enemy to our lives. He comes down to do miracles. Praise and worship draws the attention of the Almighty God to our direction. Surely, the Lord inhabits the praise of his people. Praise and worship is comely to the Lord, so make it a part of your life, church, home, and you will see the Lord taking control of that atmosphere. Another way to create an atmosphere for miracles is to have an expectant heart.

Having an Expectant Heart

For surely there is an end; and thine expectation
shall not be cut off.

—Proverbs 23:18

Expectation is very important for the birth of a
miracle. In fact, it is the bedrock for the birth of a
miracle. Rise up in the morning with the expectation
of seeing a blessed and prosperous day. It will create the
required atmosphere for a miracle. Go to work with the
expectation of meeting the company's set goals. It will
create an atmosphere for a high level of results. Go to
church with the expectation of receiving from the Lord.
It will create an atmosphere for your miracle. Great
miracles are birthed out of great expectations, and so the
flow of miracles into our lives stops whenever we stop
expecting anything from the Lord.

EXPECTATION IN THE HOUSE OF GOD

When we have nothing to expect from the Lord, we have nothing to receive. He that comes to the Lord must believe that he is and that he is a rewarder of those who diligently seek him (Hebrews 11:6). Seek God diligently. Seek to receive something from him. It will create the atmosphere for a miracle. Remember, the Lord shall not cut off the expectation of the righteous.

Today, many people go to the house of the Lord for the wrong reasons. We have people whose motive for going to the Lord is not to seek him but for personal reasons. There are people who go to the house of the Lord with no expectation, and therefore get nothing from the Lord. Such people are there because they see the church as a social club and just want to be part of that club. It is not because they expect to receive anything from God. Others are also in the house of the Lord to see the face of the man of God and not the face of God. They have probably heard about him, his name, and the great things the Lord has used him to do and decided to come see his face. To them, they are seeking to see the face of a man, not the face of the God behind the man. We also have another group of people who go to church to make contacts with other men and not to contact the God of heaven. Others are seeking to see the beauty of the sanctuary but not to behold the beauty of God's holiness.

Whenever people are in the house of the Lord for the wrong reasons, no atmosphere is created for a miracle. Where people are in a service with wrong motives, the atmosphere is nothing but spiritual dryness. The people come in and go out the same.

Personally, I realized a greater manifestation of the Holy Spirit when I ministered in churches for people with a high level of expectation than in places where the people have little or no expectations. When you visit a church or a town for a crusade where the people yearn or desire to see the glory of God, the turnout is great. The result is a strong move of the Holy Spirit, and great healings and miracles happen. However, in churches or towns where the people expect nothing from the Lord, the turnout is poor with, just a few things happening.

EXPECTATION AND FAMILIARITY WITH THE VESSEL OF GOD

And they rose early in the morning, and went forth into the wilderness of Tekoa: and as they went forth, Jehoshapat stood and said, Hear me, O Judah, and ye inhabitants of Jerusalem; Believe in the Lord your God, so shall ye be established; believe his prophets, so shall ye prosper.

—2 Chronicles 20:20

25

The way and manner we receive the ministry of a servant of God will determine the kind of blessings the Lord releases to us. A poor reception for a man of God or a poor reception for his ministry creates an unpleasant atmosphere for a miracle no matter the level of anointing upon the minister's life. It is easy for people to believe God but hard for them to believe God's Word through a man of God. I had an interesting elderly couple in my church. I was their pastor, but they could not believe the Word of God through me. They had their old pastor that they like to check with for each sermon I preached. Their main reason for doing this was because they could not fully trust me because I was a young man, and their former pastor was an old man. This kind of attitude is not conducive for anyone to receive a miracle through the ministry of their man of God. Familiarity with the man of God has also robbed many people of miracles. Jesus could do only a few miracles in his hometown, Nazareth, because the people were offended in him. They knew all about him and his family. They defined his social status as the carpenter's son instead of seeing him as a prophet and savior. It was hard for them to accept him or believe him because of what they knew about him.

> And when he was come into his own country, he taught them in their synagogue, insomuch that they were astonished, and said, Whence hath this man this wisdom, and these mighty works?

Is not this the carpenter's son? is not his mother called Mary? and his brethren, James, and Joses, and Simon, and Judas? And his sisters, are they not all with us? Whence then hath this man all these things? And they were offended in him. But Jesus said unto them, A prophet is not without honour, save in his own country, and in his own house.

And he did not many mighty works there because of their unbelief. (Matt. 13:54–58)

Whether you know a man of God from birth or you know his background or have dined with him before, it should not be a yardstick to determine the grace of God upon his life. We need to see the God behind the man of God, rather than only the man. If you cannot see the God behind him, you cannot have an open heart to receive, accept, and be blessed through his ministry. You can sit under the ministry of an anointed man of God, walk with him, or even eat with him, but if you have nothing to expect from the Lord through him, you can remain the same for many years. I had a man in my ministry who had no respect for the grace of God upon my life. He felt he had more material possessions than I did, and so in his "little" mind-set, he was more blessed than me and could not submit to my authority as his pastor. It was hard for him to call me his pastor, yet he sat under my ministry every Sunday. Meanwhile, he had a complicated ailment and needed a healing miracle. He watched with awe others receive healing through my ministry whereas he received nothing from the Lord. Though I loved him and really wished he received his healing, the God of justice will not let him. Yes, I call him the God of justice because he dispenses justice fairly and will never allow you to benefit from the ministry of a man you have no respect for. The anointing you don't respect, you don't benefit through it.

This man reminds me of the story in the Bible of Elisha and the king of Samaria's personal confidant. We are told that when the word of God came through Elisha about the end of an impending famine in the city of Samaria within a twenty-four-hour period, the king's confidant had no respect for that word from him.

> Then Elisha said, Hear ye the word of the Lord; Thus saith the Lord, Tomorrow about this time shall a measure of fine flour be sold for a shekel, and two measures of barley for a shekel, in the gate of Samaria.
>
> And it came to pass as the man of God had spoken to the king, saying, Two measures of barley for a shekel, and a measure of fine flour for a shekel, shall be tomorrow about this time in the gate of Samaria:
>
> And that lord answered the man of God, and said, Now, behold, if the LORD should make windows in heaven, might such a thing be? And he said, Behold, thou shalt see it with thine eyes, but shalt not eat thereof. (2 Kings 7:1, 17–18)

This nobleman who questioned the truth of Elisha's word saw the plenty but did not eat of it. He had no respect for Elisha's anointing and did not qualify to receive the blessing of God through him. He only saw with his eyes that blessing but was trampled on as he tried to take charge of the blessing.

If we get to a point where we stop expecting anything new through the ministry of a man of God, nothing new happens in our lives through the grace of God upon him.

LEAVING BEHIND A BLESSING

> And whosoever shall not receive you, nor hear your words, when ye depart out of that house or city, shake off the dust of your feet. (Matt. 10:14)

In the verse above, Jesus admonished his servants to shake the dust off their feet and leave no blessings in places where they are given a poor reception.

In the above scripture, Jesus is clear on who is not qualified to receive a blessing through our ministry: those who reject us or our ministry and those who oppose, resist, and reject the word of God through us.

I was holding my first conference in North Attleboro, Massachusetts. The power of God to heal was present, and people were receiving miracles with powerful prophetic directions from the Lord. We had a guy who had travelled from Worcester, Massachusetts, to be part of the meeting. He was watching all these great things happen, and instead of having an open heart to receive from the Lord, he was very skeptical and stood there an angry man. Suddenly, the Lord ministered to me about him. He had hernia and needed prayers so he might avoid going through surgical procedure for its removal. Since I didn't want to say that out loudly to the hearing of everyone at the meeting, I whispered into his ears what I had heard from the Lord. He admitted having hernia, but then said he didn't need prayers from me. I was stunned, but since I had other people waiting to be prayed for, I asked him to step aside and see me after the service. He did that, and I continued with the ministration. The service was over, and respectfully, I went to talk with him. He began challenging me, saying that he can tell me with certainty that the conference was organized in the flesh and that he was also a minister and could pray to God to heal him. Since I was not ready to get into a power struggle with him, I shook off the dust off my feet and left him with his hernia. Days later, he called for prayers for healing of the same hernia, but I didn't feel anointed at that point to deal with his issue in prayer, so he lost that miracle. So I have learnt over the years that it is not worth it to waste time on any person or group of people who are not ready to accept you, your ministry, or even the word of God through you.

Elisha left a blessing in the house of the shunammite woman only after he was accepted and received a good treatment from her. The woman was quick to recognize him as a man of God, invited him to her rich home, gave him a beautiful room to lodge, and fed him well. The man of God felt respected, appreciated, and happy with the woman—so much that he left behind for her a blessing of a baby.

> And it fell on a day, that Elisha passed to Shenum, where was a great woman; and she constrained him to eat bread. And so it was, that as oft as he passed by, he turned in thither to eat bread. And she said unto her husband, Behold now, I perceive that this is an holy man of God, which passeth by us continually. Let us make a little chamber, I pray thee, on the wall; and let us set for him there a bed, and a table, and a stool, and a candlestick: and it shall be, when he cometh to us that he shall turn in thither. And it fell on a day, that he came thither, and he turned into the chamber, and lay there. And he said to Gehazi his servant, Call this Shunammite. And when he had called her, she stood before him. And he said unto him, Say now unto her, Behold thou hast been careful for us with all care; what is to be done for thee? Wouldest thou be spoken for to the king, or to the captain of the host? And she answered, I dwell among mine own people.

And he said, What then is to be done for her? And Gehazi answered, Verily she hath no child, and her husband is old. And he said, Call her. And when he had called her, she stood in the door. And he said, About this season, according to the time of life, thou shalt embrace a son. And she said, Nay, my lord, thou man of God, do not lie unto thine hand maid. And the woman conceived, and bare a son at that season that Elisha had said unto her, according to the time of life. (2 Kings 4:8–17)

Whenever true servants of God are treated with respect and dignity, whether in our homes, at a dinner table, or invited to preach in our churches, they leave behind a blessing for us in the end. I made a decision some years ago that our ministry was not going to bring to the church a guest speaker if we did not have enough funds to cater for his stay and see him off with some good honorarium. My wife and I also made a decision that we were not going to receive into our home any guest unless we were in a position to make the person's stay with us a memorable one.

He that receiveth a prophet in the name of a prophet shall receive a prophet's reward; and he that receiveth a righteous man in the name of a righteous man shall receive a righteous man's reward. (Mathew 10:41)

There is something called a prophet reward. It is a blessing reserved by heaven for true servants of God to leave behind for whosoever receives and treats them well. God never specified what that blessing is and what measure should be left behind. He left that decision to be determined by his servants as led by the Holy Spirit.

EXPECTATION AND PRAYER

Let us therefore come boldly unto the throne of grace that we may obtain mercy, and find grace to help in time of need.

—Hebrews 4:16

Our time of need in life could turn out to be our time of discouragement too. It is a time when most people fix their eyes on the need instead of mustering courage to present our petitions and supplication to God in prayer. When we come boldly to God and present our needs while at the same time expecting the answers from him, he releases mercy and grace for the performance of a miracle. Otherwise, it is a waste of time and senseless bombardment of heaven with our prayers.

I have seen people who started complaints about the very issues they just finished praying about. It is a sign of a lack of expectation when that happens. How could someone who just finished thanking God for answering his prayer and saying *amen* suddenly turn around to complain about what he believes has been answered by the Lord?

Years ago, my wife and I had a major financial obligation to meet by a certain deadline. As the date drew near, we realized we did not have enough money to meet the deadline. A day before the date, we prayed about it together before she left for work. While by myself, I had a deep intuition that somehow God was going to cause the release of some money from somewhere to meet that need. I simply had expectation of receiving a miracle from the Lord. That day, I checked our bank accounts online over and over for any new deposit, but nothing had changed. I checked the mailbox for the letters for that day, but there was no letter with any good news than our usual bills.

Shortly after picking up the mail for that day, I received a phone call from a friend. He wanted to drop by for a discussion. I was not expecting anything from him, but you never know. The Lord knows no limits. He is able to use anyone to meet a need. The guy arrived, but the purpose of his visit was to receive prayers for some challenges he was dealing with. In the middle of our discussion, my wife arrived from work. I excused him and went in to talk with her. Before I could find out how her day went, she showed me a check as big as the amount we needed. It was the exact amount of money we needed to meet that financial obligation. The Lord had placed a burden upon the heart of a lady, a family friend, to bless her with that check. It was unbelievable the way heaven responded quickly. God is real, and there is no end to what He can do! That check was the release of a miracle through the power of prayer and expectation.

Jesus always asked people what their expectations were before touching their need. He knew all men. He knew their problems, and yet he always wanted to know their expectations. Once he met two blind men (Matt. 20:29–34). They cried out aloud, saying, "Have mercy on us, O Lord, Son of David." The multitude around Jesus warned them to be quiet, but they were adamant. Finally, Jesus stood still, called them, and said, "What do you want me to do for you?" The men said to him, "Lord, that our eyes may be healed." Jesus had compassion on them and touched their eyes, and immediately, their eyes received sight.

The blindness of these two men was glaringly obvious. Jesus heard them crying to him to have mercy on them. It was clear by their actions that they had a pressing need. Their aim was to get the attention of Jesus. They cried for mercy, persisted until they were heard by the Lord, and finally caught the attention of the Master. Did Jesus assume their need? He made no assumption at all. He questioned what they expected from him. Then as the men told him their expectation, he went ahead and healed them.

Your expectation will create the required atmosphere for a miracle. The woman with the issue of blood had a high expectation that as long as she was able to touch the hem of the Lord's garment, she would get healed. That expectation created the atmosphere for her miracle. She touched the Lord's garment, and much to her surprise, she received her miracle (Matt. 9:20–22). Your expectation will connect you to the treasures of heaven.

EXPECTATION AND THE PULL OF VIRTUE

And a certain woman which had an issue of blood twelve years, And had suffered many things of many physicians, and had spent all she had, and was nothing bettered, but rather grew worse. When she had heard of Jesus, came in the press behind, and touched his garment. For she said, If I may touch but his clothes, I shall be whole. And straightway the fountain of her blood was dried up; and she felt in her body that she was healed of that plague. And Jesus, immediately knowing that virtue had gone out of him, turned him about in the press, and said, Who touched my clothes?

—Mark 5:25–30(KJV)

Your expectation can help you tap into the anointing of a man of God from a distance. The two blind men mentioned in Mathew 20:29–34 brought Jesus to a standstill from a distance through the power of expectation. There were multitudes around Jesus with various needs, but despite their closeness to the Master, they could not tap into His anointing because of their low level of expectation. However, this woman with the issue of blood, through a high level of expectation, drew virtue out of Jesus from behind. You can pull virtue out of a man of God through the power of expectation. In a church service, it is not the kind of seat you sit on or your location that draws God's attention to you but the expectation you came to the service with. I have seen people who sat at the front row, close to the pulpit and to the man of God, receive nothing while others who sat at the back pews caught the attention of God. So for a miracle to happen, the expectation of what you want to receive from God matters.

In my ministry, I have seen people draw virtue from me from behind. It happens in a way that while I am ministering at a service, someone at the back row, hidden in the congregation, suddenly catches my attention. Thus, his expectation causes a pull of virtue out of me. That person is able to catch my attention and the attention of God because he came to the service with a high expectation of being blessed through my ministry. He came to the meeting with just one prayer—that the Lord might use me to touch his life. That strong expectation for a blessing through my ministry was what caused a pull of virtue out of me. When that happens, you will see me bypass everyone in the service and head for that person.

In 2010, I was ministering in a church in Maryland in the United States, and at some point, I called out the sick for prayers. One lady was among those who stepped out. She was not sick, but she came to stand in the gap for a friend diagnosed with cancer. She had high expectations that her friend would get healed through my ministry. Before I was there for that program, she and her friend had talked about this man of God (referring to me) who was coming from Boston, Massachusetts, to her church to hold a service. Her friend had told her how doctors had diagnosed her with cancer, but she'd assured her she would be standing in the gap to receive prayers for her healing during the program.

I had no prior knowledge of all this discussion, and she had not mentioned it to me. When it got to her turn for prayers, she told me she was standing in the gap for a friend. I prayed for the friend with the cancer, using her as a point of contact. A month after the prayers, I was on the highway, driving from Boston to Plainville, when I received a text message from the sister. She had a praise report about her friend for whom she stood for prayers. She has been healed from the cancer. She went for a biopsy after the prayers, and the result was negative. The cancer has disappeared. Surely, Jesus sent forth His word and healed her disease. There is no distance in the spirit.

The people who benefit from the anointing of God upon my life are those who have an expectation to receive through my ministry. They are people who have value for the grace of God upon my life. Remember you can never benefit from an anointing you don't respect.

In 1998, I was ministering at a service in Ghana and being led by the Holy Spirit. I took off my shoes and laid them on the floor. There were some people at that meeting who had a high expectation of receiving from God through my ministry. They had a belief that they would get a breakthrough by just touching my shoes. As they reached out and touched it, they got slain by the fire of the Holy Spirit. Some were thrown to the floor, crying uncontrollably with loud voices as demons fled. Others became drunk in the power of the Holy Spirit and lay on the floor, unconscious.

For any miracle to happen, your expectation matters. It draws virtue from a man of God. It taps into the treasures of heaven.

Another thing that hinders us from receiving a miracle is living in an atmosphere of unforgiveness and bitterness.

UNFORGIVENESS AND BITTERNESS

For if ye forgive men their trespasses, your heavenly Father will also forgive you: But if ye forgive not men their trespasses, neither will your Father forgive your trespasses.

—Matthew 6:14–15(KJV)

No atmosphere for miracles is created when people live in unforgiveness and bitterness. An unhealthy spiritual atmosphere is created when two people sitting next to each other in a church or at work are bitter with one another and cannot simply forgive each other. The spiritual atmosphere gets poisoned and stinks like hydrogen sulfide when leaders and their pastor or a boss and his subordinates get bitter with each other beyond forgiveness.

UNFORGIVENESS CAUSES
A PUNGENT SPIRITUAL ATMOSPHERE

One day as I was preparing a sermon on unforgiveness and bitterness for a Sunday morning service, the Lord revealed to me that unforgiveness and bitterness usually creates a kind of spiritual atmosphere comparable to that of hydrogen sulfide being released in an environment. I said, "Well, I had never thought about it that way, Lord, but now I know." With my background as a mineral engineer, I knew exactly the kind of picture the Lord wanted to show me; this was the best way he could help me understand the subject matter of bitterness and unforgiveness. For those who might not have any idea about this gas called hydrogen sulfide, I will help you understand its characteristics.

It is a dangerous gas with a pungent smell. Typically, it smells like a rotten egg, and once released in an environment, the smell gets so bad that you will not want to hang around that atmosphere for a second. It drives everyone away. Such is the kind of spiritual atmosphere created around us when we live in bitterness and unforgiveness. That kind of atmosphere drives away God and is dangerous to men.

I mentioned in one of my previous books *Wonders of Peace* about a church that was not experiencing numerical growth for many years all because of a long-standing dispute between the worship leader and another leader of the church. All evangelism steps embarked upon to bring growth to the church failed, and nobody understood what was going on with the church. In just one day, the worship leader, with a trembling voice, took the blame and apologized to the other leader before the congregation. Shortly after this incident, the veil of darkness over the church was lifted, and the church experienced tremendous growth.

In the same way, where there is conflict in an organization between workers or people at the hem of affairs, setback is inevitable, and little result is achievable. One of the major obligations of every CEO is to help create a healthy working relationship among workers and leaders. It will create a good atmosphere for a miracle of growth and productivity.

Bitterness and unforgiveness creates a distasteful atmosphere for the Lord and makes it impossible for any miracle to happen. God considers bitterness and unforgiveness a serious issue. It brings a veil of darkness around an environment. He has warned us that whenever we fail to forgive someone their trespasses against us, he will also not forgive us our trespasses against him. Think about it! And if the Lord is holding your trespasses against you, how will he release a miracle to you? He questioned, "If we cannot love our brother, whom we live with, how can we claim to love God, whom we cannot see" (1 John 4:20). Simply put, the Lord is saying that we are behaving like hypocrites if we cannot live with our fellow beings in a spirit of love and yet claim to love him. If you cannot love your pastor, why go to church to listen to his powerful sermons every Sunday? And if as a pastor you cannot love a church member, why carry the Bible to preach to him anyway?

God is calling upon the church, families, and everyone to get back to the principles of love. Love covers a multitude of sins. Love suffers long and is kind. Love does not envy, does not parade itself, and is not puffed up. Love does not behave rudely, does not seek its own, is not provoked, thinks no evil, does not rejoice in iniquity but rejoices in the truth, bears all things, believes all things, hopes all things, and endures all things.

UNFORGIVENESS CAUSES SPIRITUAL CRISIS

The church is in a spiritual crisis today because of bitterness and unforgiveness. When a few people in church feel things are not done their way, they will not voice their concerns but stage a rebellion against the pastor and stop supporting the church with their tithes and offering. Their next action is to start a new church. Afterward, they try to justify their actions by castigating their former pastor, painting their former church and pastor black and making all efforts to pull away the few folks left in that church. This is not love. It is rebellion! And the Lord's place for the rebellious is the land of dryness.

When people receive a rebuke and correction from the pastor of a church for committing abominable sins, their next option is to form an alliance with some few innocent folks in the church and stage a conspiracy against the pastor. They will say all sorts of dirty lies about the pastor to score a point all because they could not get their way. Be careful!

You cannot touch the Lord's anointed and be free. Your days on earth could be cut by half. Everything around you could come under crisis because of touching the Lord's anointed. The Lord can hit your life with spiritual leprosy.

When there is unforgiveness and bitterness among members, leaders, and the pastor in a church, a spiritual crisis will hit the church, and the Lord will withhold his blessings. When there is bitterness between a married couple, a spiritual crisis will hit the marriage. When the pastor of the church is despised, disrespected, and given poor treatment by the church members and leaders, the Lord will withhold his blessings. Church leaders and members will do everything possible to please a visiting preacher but not their pastor. That too can let God withhold his blessings. Remember Jesus did not do many miracles in his hometown because the people were offended at him. They were used to him. They knew him as the carpenter's son and a nonentity. His familiarity with them led to contempt for him and robbed them of the miracles they should have received through him. Whenever we develop contempt for a man of God because of our familiarity with him, it becomes hard if not impossible to receive a miracle through his ministry.

One time, a great man of God went to preach in another church. The church was a big one. The leaders were wealthy and happy people, but the pastor was poor-looking, rejected, and frustrated. Here were the leaders of the church in expensive traditional and western dresses, whereas the pastor wore kingpin khaki pants with an old-looking shirt.

The first night of that program, the Holy Spirit refused to move. The visiting pastor in question is a highly anointed man of God, and wherever he stands to minister, the Lord confirms his Word through him with signs and wonders, but that night, the Lord refused to move. Attendees of the program and the guest speaker himself left the service with dashed hopes and expectations. The man of God got to his hotel room, confused. Shedding tears, he wondered why the Holy Spirit did not move. He was scared that the Holy Spirit has probably left him. He prayed hard before the Lord, asking him questions. Finally the Lord whispered to him his reason for not releasing blessings that night.

The problem was the pastor of the church. I'm sure you are surprised and wondering at this point why the Holy Spirit refused to move that night because of the resident pastor. The reason is that this pastor was struggling so hard financially, whereas the leaders of the church were having good times and enjoying with their families. Apparently, the Lord was not pleased with this kind of treatment meted out to his servant and simply withheld his blessings. That night, the visiting pastor asked the Lord what to do, and he (Lord) gave him instructions to raise an offering solely for the resident pastor in the next service. The next night, before delivering his sermon, he requested a special offering from the congregation without telling them what it was to be used for. The leaders of the church were writing big checks, and people donated big sums of money. The visiting pastor then handed all that money to the resident pastor. With joy and surprise, the pastor received it, and the visiting pastor continued his sermon. And that night, the spiritual crisis turned into a spiritual crossover for the people. The heavens kissed the earth, and unusual miracles happened.

I was invited to preach in a certain church in the United States. I prepared myself in prayers. I was excited that God was going to do great things in that church, but as I was on board the plane, I had an unusual intuition about the church. I was wondering what that could be, but the Lord soon showed me that unforgiveness and bitterness has gripped the pastor, leaders, and members of the church. Simply put, the church was in a spiritual crisis.

I was willing to see the Lord do his usual healing and miracles through me, but it did not happen that much. The response was poor, and we did not register much result for that program. I broke down in my hotel room. I was in tears about the way unforgiveness and bitterness had gripped people of the church in our day.

UNFORGIVENESS CAUSES MARRIAGE CRISIS

And this have ye done again, covering the altar of the Lord with tears, with weeping, and with crying out, insomuch that he regarded not the offering any more, or receiveth it with good will at your hand. Yet ye say, wherefore? Because the Lord hath been witness between thee and the wife of thy youth, against whom thou has dealt treacherously, yet is she thy companion, and the wife of thy covenant.

—Malachi 2:13–14

Dealing treacherously with your partner in marriage and refusing to forgive and let go of offenses can cause the Lord to close the heavens to our prayers. When bitterness and unforgiveness grips a family, the family gets into crisis. God withholds his blessings from that home and family. Don't be ignorant of the devices of the devil. Give him no place in your home. Avoid bitterness and unforgiveness.

Married couples should settle their differences as soon as possible. As much as possible, pursue peace and create joy at home. Share the success and failures of your day and have fun. Don't capitalize on your partner's weakness and abuse him or her daily with that. Instead, help him or her work on that weakness. Major on your partner's strength and help develop it.

Marriage is sweet but can turn bitter if not handled well and properly. It can be heaven or hell depending on how a couple handles it. It can be the source of crisis or a blessing in a man's life. So make your choice this day which way you want to go, but I encourage you to go for the heaven and blessing part of a marriage.

Another way to create an atmosphere for miracles is to be responsive to the Word of God.

BEING RESPONSIVE TO THE WORD OF GOD

We need to be responsive to the Word of God that is preached to us. It will create an atmosphere for miracles. We show our irresponsiveness to the Word of God when we have no reverence for it, resist it, harden our hearts to it, or allow traditions in our lives and in the church.

REVERENCE FOR THE WORD OF GOD

And he read therein before the street that was before the water gate from the morning until midday, before the men and the women, and those that could understand; and the ears of all the people were attentive unto the book of the law.
And Ezra the scribe stood upon a pulpit of wood, which they had made for the purpose; and beside

him Mattithiah, and Shema, and Anaiah, and
Urijah, and Hilkiah, and Maaseiah, on his right,
on his right hand, and on his left hand, Pedaiah,
and Mishael, and Malchiah, and Hashum and
Hashbadana, Zechariah, and Mesullam.
And Ezra opened the book in the sight of all the
people; (for he was above all the people;) and
when he opened it, all the people stood up. And
Ezra blessed the Lord, the great God. And all
the people answered, Amen, Amen, with lifting
up of their hands: and they bowed their heads,
and worshipped the Lord with their faces to the
ground.

—Nehemiah 8:3–5 (KJV)

Don't be tired of listening to the Word of God. Stay
alert and attentive when it is preached to you. That will
create an atmosphere for miracles. The Word of God is
holy and must be revered. We do not show reverence to
his Word when we sleep, engage in a conversation, or
chew gum while it is preached. Engaging in such actions
is a clear disrespect for the Word of God. We create an
atmosphere for miracles when we tremble at the Word
of God. It is recorded in the Bible that God has exalted
his Word above his name, and if he has, then we need to
exalt it also. It is therefore a sign of irresponsiveness to
the Word of God when people are engaged in something
else in the church while the Word is preached. That

does not create an atmosphere for miracles. It only distracts the move of the Holy Spirit, who is behind the miraculous acts of God.

In the days of Ezra, the children of Israel listened with rapt attention from morning till noonday as the Word of God was read by Ezra. When Ezra opened the book of the Lord, the people stood up as a way of reverence for the Word of God. As Ezra blessed the name of the Lord, the people lifted up their hands and heads to worship the Lord. All these were acts done by the people in reverence to the Word of God.

We can stand up in reverence to the Word of God as it is preached to us. We can lift up our hands in reverence to the Word of God as we receive it. We can even bow down and worship the Lord as the Word is preached to us. It will create the required atmosphere for a miracle to happen. When we walk away from a preacher while a sermon is delivered, it does not show reverence for the Word of God and grieves the Holy Spirit. The move of God is killed. When we distract the preacher's attention through our movement in a service, it creates an unhealthy atmosphere for any miracle.

RESISTING THE WORD OF GOD

Then there arose certain of the synagogue, which is called the synagogue of the Libertines, and

the Cyrenians, and Alexandrians, and of them
Cilicia and of Asia, disputing with Stephen. And
they were not able to resist the wisdom and the
spirit by which he spake.

—Acts 6:9–10(KJV)

When we cannot receive a sermon from a preacher as
the Word of God, we are resisting the Word. When
people sit in church and "pass" the Word of God to other
people instead of receiving it as a personal word from
the Lord, they are resisting the Word of God. When the
Word is preached with power and it cuts the heart of
people, it is just proper to accept it and repent. Instead,
some people misinterpret it and say that the pastor is
preaching about them. That is a resistance to the Word
of God. People resist the Word of God and fight it when
it reproves something sinful in their lives. Some resist it
when it is not preached their way. It must be their way,
or it is rejected. I have heard people say they accept the
New Testament but not the Old Testament. Anything
preached from the Old Testament is given an outright
rejection. The Word of God must be acceptable wholly,
whether from the New or Old Testament, in order for
us to be blessed through it. We are told in 2 Timothy
3:16 that every scripture is inspired by God and useful
for teaching, for reproof, for correction, and for training
in righteousness. So it is not in our power to decide

which part of the Bible to accept or reject. The worst part of resisting the Word of God is to claim the Bible has errors.

I had a Christian brother who had a roll of problems in almost every area of his life. It was one problem after another until I decided one day to have a serious counseling session for both him and the wife together. Something unbelievable came up during that session, and I understood why the brother was going through the confusion in his life. He had a problem with the Bible as the true and authoritative word of God. He believed it has thousands of errors and that he was not getting any break in life because he was using the name *Jesus* instead of *Yeshua* (Hebrew name for the Son of God) in his prayers. He also claimed that the right name for God is Jehovah and that the use of the word *God* to refer to Jehovah was like mistakenly calling a man named John as Andrew. I spent time trying to get him to understand things more clearly, but he held on to his beliefs and started spreading those wrong beliefs among some members of the church. So I had no option than advice him to find another church. That settled the matter.

There is also another group of people who resist the Word of God by fighting the vessel that God uses to deliver his Word to them. Such people see it as a man's word instead of God's Word through a man. They resist the Word of God just like how the people of the synagogue of the Libertines, Cyrenians, and others resisted Stephen when he preached the Word of God with power. They were unable to resist the wisdom and the spirit by which he spoke and instead of repenting, they resisted the Word of God and stoned him to death.

Today, many pastors are being blackmailed and castigated for preaching the Word of God when it directly or indirectly affects somebody's evil lifestyle. Such people will resist God's Word through a pastor by refusing to attend his church or refusing to support the work of God with their tithes and offering, or, worse, they stir up a conspiracy in the church against the pastor. This is our modern way of stoning the pastor and his ministry to death.

> When they heard these things, they were cut to the heart, and they gnashed on him with their teeth. (Acts 7:54, KJV)

Many churches have broken down. Membership, as well as tithes, disintegrates from big numbers to small numbers just because the servant of God delivered a sermon that reproved someone. Our generation has itching ears and wants to hear what is suitable to their ears and not what is suitable to the ears of God. You can only draw a great crowd to your church when you preach inspiring and ear-itching exhortations every Sunday.

56

People will love you and call you a good pastor then. They will give you all the support you need as long as you don't preach about the no-go areas of their lives. It is so serious that many pastors have stopped preaching about holiness. Our generation is not ready for any sermon on holiness and will resist such sermons from a pastor with all their might and to their fullest ability.

When the Word of God comes and exposes your sins, accept it and repent in tears instead of trying to fight back; otherwise, you will only end up in spiritual or physical death. The Lord warned Saul (now Paul) that it was a hard thing to kick against the pricks. In other words, God warned Saul that he could not resist him or his Word and prevail. Again, God warned the children of Israel through his prophet Hosea that he would not release his blessings to his people, who rejected his Word (Hos. 4:6).

Whenever people resist the Word of God, we create an unpleasant atmosphere for a miracle because in that Word is the totality of every blessing we need. Whenever our hearts cannot receive the Word of God, then the move of God is blocked.

ELISHA AND THE KING'S ASSISTANT

One time, when there was famine in the land of Samaria, God used his servant Elisha to prophesy a twenty-four-hour miracle of abundance of food on the land, but an assistant to the king resisted the Word of God through Elisha. He said to the man of God, "That could not happen even if the Lord opened the windows of heaven." But Elisha replied, "You will see it, but you will be able to eat of it" (2 Kings 7:1–2).

In the later verses, specifically 2 Kings 7:16–20, the Word of the Lord through Elisha is fulfilled, but the assistant to the king is not able to enjoy the blessing through the Word of God he resisted and rejected. The people trod upon him in the gate as he tried to take charge of the blessing.

What were his reasons for resisting and rejecting the Word of God? First of all, he thought it was man's word, and not the Word of the Lord through a man. Secondly, he was using his natural mind to assess the situation. After all, he was an assistant to the king and had enough information available to him about the severity of the famine. He thought to himself that the economic indicators were very bad and that there was no way a twenty-four-hour economic turnaround could happen. "That is impossible!" he probably exclaimed. We are not told what role he served as an officer in the palace of the king, but his response to the Word of God and the fact that the King appointed him to take charge of the economic situation and food management when the Word of God was fulfilled suggests that he might have knowledge in finance and economic planning. A third reason why he resisted the Word of God was because he undermined the provision of God. He said that even if God opened the windows of heaven, there was no way such a miracle of an abundance of food could happen. Simply put, he was saying not even God was capable of getting them out of that deep economic crisis. Therefore, he did not believe in what he thought were fake prophecies. He labeled Elisha as a false prophet, a liar, one who probably wanted to gain favor from the king by just giving him false words of encouragement.

Today, just like this assistant to the king, many people have labeled men of God as liars and false prophets. They say, "That pastor says God will do this and that in my life, but you know what? I cannot imagine that happening under the situation I am in now. I am not sure that is the way God works! It's all a lie!"

Through these excuses and buts, we end up resisting the Word of God and the man of God as well. But over and over, I realize the very Word of God men resist and reject is what carries the blessing they need or desire to have in life. When you reject the Word of God on healing, it becomes hard to receive a healing miracle from God. When you reject the Word of God on prosperity, the chains of poverty and lack will hold you bound. Jesus said, "You shall know the truth [the Word] and the truth will set you free" (John 8:32). It is God's Word that sets us free from the bondage and chains of Satan.

Do not assess God with your carnal mind. His ways are different from the ways of man. His thoughts are higher that our thoughts, and it is impossible to predict what God is able to do in the next few seconds. Resist the temptation of allowing the situations around you to decide the plan of God for your life.

THE HEALING PROCESS OF NAAMAN

Then Naaman went with his horses and chariot, and he stood at the door of Elisha's house. And Elisha sent a messenger to him, saying, "Go and wash in the Jordan seven times, and your flesh shall be restored to you, and you shall be clean". But Naaman became furious, and went away and said, "Indeed, I said to myself, 'He will surely come out to me and stand and call on the name of the Lord his God, and wave his hand over the place, and heal the leprosy.' Are not the Abanah and the Pharpar, the rivers of Damascus, better than all the waters of Israel? Could I not wash in them and be clean?" So he turned and went away in a rage. And his servants came near and spoke to him, and said, "My father, if the prophet had told you to do something great, would you not have done it? How much more then, when he says to you, 'Wash, and be clean? So he went down and dipped seven times in the Jordan, according to the saying of the man of God; and his flesh was restored like the flesh of a little child, and he was clean. (2 Kings 5:9–14)

Naaman's reason for going to Elisha was to receive healing. It did not matter whether the man of God laid hands on him for that healing or asked him to wash in the Jordan River seven times. What was most important in this account was his healing. He should have simply accepted the Word of God and acted on it, but the case is different here.

First of all, he was furious with the man of God for his method of delivery. He expected him to come out, give him a hearty welcome, and then wave his hand over the spot with leprosy, but it did not happen that way. Instead, he was asked by the man of God to do something very simple for his healing—bathe in the river Jordan. The right atmosphere for a miracle is created when we go before God or appear before a man of God with our minds open to receiving something from the Lord, however he chooses to do it. Sometimes, the Holy Spirit might lead the servant of the Lord to lay hands, and sometimes he might choose anointing with oil. Other times, the man of God might just deliver a word and, in some instances, give simple counseling. Whichever way the Lord chooses to go, we are supposed to follow his leading. All we need to do is come to God with a humble and open mind. We should not be prejudiced on God's method of delivery. Don't appear in God's presence with this attitude that you know how God will work through his servant. You can miss your miracle with that kind of mind-set.

Second, the Word of God did not appear to make sense to Naaman. He despised it. He would have discarded it immediately but for the persuasion from his servants to humble himself and act on the Word of God. He said to himself, "Why will bathing in a river like Jordan make me whole? See, I have better rivers in my country than that river."

Sometimes, the Word of God from a man of God might not appear to make sense to us, but we still need to humbly accept it because even the foolishness of God is wiser that the wisdom of men. Even if it is not what you want to hear, accept it and act on it.

Naaman's actions showed his arrogance and resistance to the Word of God. He went to God with an attitude of "it must be this way and not that way. The Word of the Lord must be my way, not God's way." When we have this kind of attitude, we are resisting the Word of God, and an atmosphere for a miracle is hindered. Remember, there is no methodology when it comes to how God works. His ways are different from our ways and far from our understanding.

THE DISCIPLES' MIRACULOUS CATCH OF FISH

There is a blessing in responding to the Word of God. Peter and the disciples fished all night and caught no fish, but when they acted upon the instruction of Jesus to cast their net into the sea again, they had had such a miraculous and huge catch of fish.

HARDENING OUR HEARTS TO THE WORD OF GOD

And they come unto thee as the people cometh, and they sit before thee as my people, and they hear thy words, but they will not do them: for with their mouth they shew much, but they heart goeth after their covetousness.

—Ezekiel 33:31(KJV)

God's Word is living and powerful. It is sharper than any two-edged sword. It pierces the joints and marrow, and even the division of the soul and spirit. It is powerful enough to quicken the dead, but when a man's heart is hardened, the Word of God has no power to affect his life. Preach the Word of God over and over to a man with a hardened heart, and it will make no sense to him.

The Word has no place in his heart. He will listen to you preach but then says in his heart, "I hear you. I know that's what the Lord says, but I am not ready to go that way." To such a person, the Word has no power to convict his heart. He is only a hearer of the Word of God and not a doer. In an environment where people harden their hearts toward God's Word, it becomes very difficult for any miracle to happen. The end is nothing but a waste of time and frustration. It is unbelievable Noah spent many years preaching about God's intention of destroying the earth through flood, yet no one listened to him. That is how it is like dealing with people having a hardened heart. We must allow the Word of God to penetrate our hearts if we desire to see an atmosphere for miracles.

A man of God once said that no amount of exhortation moves any member of his church to increase their level of giving. They look at you funny as you deliver your exhortation on giving and say in their hearts, "Whether you preach or not, nothing can change my mind about how much I want to give." And that is how people with a hardened heart behave. They can even mock you as you deliver the Word of God. Jesus talked about how Noah was mocked in his day as he delivered his message of destruction of the earth through floods. Not even one person repented after his sermons.

DWELLING ON TRADITIONS

> But he answered and said unto them, why do
> ye also transgress the commandment of God
> by your traditions...Thus have ye made the
> commandment of God of none effect by your
> tradition.
>
> —Matthew 15:3, 6 (KJV)

When we allow traditions to rule in our lives or in the
church, we make the Word of God null and void and
give no room for a miracle to happen. People who dwell
on traditions resist change even when the Lord wants it.
They hold so tight to that which has been passed down
to them by ancestors or predecessors and are not ready
to adapt to anything new. The Pharisees were one group
of people who dwelt on tradition. They believed in the
doctrine of Moses and held fast to it but were not ready
for the teachings of Jesus. Simply put, they were not
ready for change from God. Those ruled by traditions
will quote the way things were done in the past and how
others are doing it now but not how the Holy Spirit
wants it done. They are interested in maintaining the
status quo and nothing else. Traditions have killed many
churches and impeded a lot of people from receiving
their miracle. It has killed the fire of God in many
lives and churches. Jesus rebuked the Pharisees of his

day for allowing traditions to rule their lives instead of depending on the Word of God. As children of God, we are supposed to be led by the Word of God and by his Spirit, but when we hold tight to traditions, we give no room for the Holy Spirit. Eventually, he leaves our lives alone. He leaves the church.

In order to create an atmosphere for miracles, the Holy Spirit needs a place in our lives, churches, and homes because when he is kicked out, there is no way a miracle can happen around us. I have seen pastors booted out of churches for trying to follow the leading of the Holy Spirit instead of following the traditions of the church. Traditions cannot supersede the leading of the Holy Spirit. When this becomes the case in a church, the Holy Spirit quietly leaves and allows the church to be ruled with human ideas and philosophy. There and then, the fire in the church is quenched.

Another way to create an atmosphere for miracles is to dwell together in unity.

Dwelling Together in Unity

Behold, how good and how pleasant it is for brethren to dwell together in unity. It is like the precious ointment upon the head that ran down upon the beard even Aaron's beard: that went down to the skirts of his garments. As the dew of Hermon, and as the dew that descended upon the mountains of Zion: for there the Lord commanded the blessing, even life forever.

—Psalm 133:1–3 (KJV)

It is good in the sight of God when brethren dwell together in unity. A pleasant environment is created for a miracle when the bond of unity exists among brethren. When a people of a church or family are united, the Lord pours upon them His precious oil, from the head of the church, and even to the least. He pours down His favor and then commands His blessing upon them.

When a couple is united, it becomes very difficult for the devil to break into that marriage, and the couple will surely experience great miracles because of the bond of unity in the marriage.

Dwelling together in unity with one accord, vision, purpose, and goal is one of the keys for the miracle of growth and multiplication. I have never seen any organization experience growth in a condition of disunity. Absolutely nothing will fail in the hands of any group of people bound by the cord of unity.

At the time that Tower of Babel was being built, the Almighty God confessed that nothing could stop the people from achieving their aim of erecting a tower to reach the heavens simply because they were a united people with one language.

> And they said one to another, Go to, let us build us a city and a tower, whose top may reach unto heaven, and let us make us a name, lest we be scattered abroad upon the face of the whole earth.
>
> And the Lord came down to see the city and the tower, which the children of men builded. And the Lord said, Behold, the people are one, and they have all one language, and this they begin to do: and now nothing will be restrained from them, which they have imagined to do. (Gen. 11:4–6, KJV)

The spirit of oneness creates the required atmosphere for a miracle to happen. It is such a strong spirit that nothing can resist or stand it. Jesus stated that a kingdom divided cannot stand but will surely come to desolation. If the people of a kingdom are one, however, they will receive the full backing of heaven, and the required atmosphere for miracles will be seen.

The early church experienced tremendous multiplication and addition because they were of one heart and one soul. None said that any of the things he possessed was his own. They shared all things. The bond of unity was so strong that all who possessed lands or houses sold them and brought the proceeds of the things sold and laid it at the apostles' feet for distribution to all in need. That created an atmosphere for multiplication and addition of souls to the church. That broke the yoke of poverty over members of the church. It is recorded that no one lacked in the church in the early days (Acts 4:34).

When a church is united, members are willing to break bread and share things. When a church is united, members will invest their resources toward the vision of the church and support one another, and then tremendous miracles begin to happen. Certainly, unity is a necessary ingredient for a miracle, growth, or multiplication to happen.

Another way to create an atmosphere for miracles is to create a beautiful and orderly environment around us.

CREATING ORDER AND A BEAUTIFUL ENVIRONMENT

Order and a beautiful environment are things that can create an atmosphere for miracles. When things are done in an orderly manner at home or in a church, it creates an atmosphere for the Holy Spirit to move. When there is order at the work site, a good atmosphere is created for increased productivity. An environment with a high level of disorderliness creates nothing but distress and loss of productivity.

Jesus commanded the multitudes to sit down before the miracle of the multiplication of the two fishes and five loaves to feed four thousand people happened. Order was required for that miracle to happen.

> But He said to them" How many loaves do you have? Go and see". And when they found out, they said, five and two fish". Then He commanded

them to make them all sit down in groups on the green grass. So, they sat down in ranks, in hundreds and in fifties.

And when He had taken the five loaves and the two fish, He looked up to Heaven, blessed and broke the loaves, and gave them to His disciples to set before them, and the two fish He divided among them all. (Mark 6:38–41, KJV)

If there is no order in a setting, no atmosphere for a miracle is created, and no growth will occur. If you have no regard for order, then you have nothing to do with having a miracle.

The Queen of Sheba praised King Solomon for the orderly setting of his palace. She was humbled not only by King Solomon's wisdom but also by the level of order in his palace.

And when the queen of Sheba had seen all Solomon's wisdom and the house that he had built, And the meat of his table, and the sitting of his servants, and the attendance of his ministers, and their apparel, and his cupbearers, and his ascent by which he went up unto the house of the Lord; there was no more spirit in her. (1 Kings 10:4–5, KJV)

The sovereign God himself is a God of order. He demonstrated his love for order at the beginning of creation. We are told in Genesis 1:2 that the earth and the heavens were without form, that they were void and in darkness. It was simply in a state of disorder and confusion, but the Lord began putting everything in a perfect order. Today, we can attest to the orderly nature of God's creation. He made the day and the night, the morning and evening, and then divided the light from the darkness. He separated the sea from the land. He made everything beautiful and orderly. The Bible says that everything He made was good.

God loves order, and anytime there is order, an atmosphere for miracles is created. We cannot expect miracles in our homes when everything is in a mess. We cannot expect miracles in a church with no order and decorum. We cannot increase productivity at work in an environment of disorder. My personal observation is that people love to hang around environments with order, but they will run away from a messy environment.

Order and a beautiful environment go together. They are both important requirements for the creation of an environment for a miracle. It is often said that cleanliness is next to godliness. We must therefore keep our environment in a state of beauty. It attracts the presence of God. It attracts people to that environment.

One thing that enhances the miracle of church growth is a beautiful environment. There are times people are drawn to a particular church, organization, or home for no other reason than for its complex architectural design and beautiful environment. Beauty enhances the flow of people to an environment.

God visited Adam and Eve in the cool of the day in a beautiful environment made of precious minerals. It was a daily visit, not a monthly or yearly one. Make your prayer closet beautiful, and it can draw God there. Make the sanctuary of your church beautiful. You will see people attracted there. Make the environment of your home beautiful. You will have a sound mind. A healthy mind is found in a healthy body living in a healthy environment.

When King Solomon built a temple for the Lord, it was indeed a beautiful one. The foundation was made of costly stones. The beams and wood were made of cedar, and the vessels for the temple were made of gold. The altar was made of gold, and the table for the showbread was also made of gold. Nothing in that temple was anything cheap; all was beautiful and costly (1 Kings 7:1–51).

> And he garnished the house with precious stones for beauty: and gold was gold of Parvaim. He overlaid also the house, the beams, the posts, and the walls thereof, and the doors thereof, with gold; and graved cherubims on the walls.
>
> And he made the most holy house, the length whereof was according to the breadth of the

house, twenty cubits, and he overlaid it with fine gold, amounting to six hundred talents. (2 Chron. 3:6–8, KJV)

The Bible records that at the time of dedication of this temple, the glory of God was so strong that the priest could not stand to minister (2 Chron. 5:14).

As I conclude on this subject, it is my prayer that the words of this book will find a place in your heart and usher you into the miracles of God

About the Book

Miracles do not come out of the blue. A suitable atmosphere is required for the Lord to work miracles in our everyday life.

In this book, you will discover the secrets to creating that perfect and suitable atmosphere for receiving unending miracles from the Lord.

You will be eternal gratefully to God for placing this precious book in your hands.